The Feudal System Uncovered

Children's Medieval History Books

Speedy Publishing LLC
40 E. Main St. #1156
Newark, DE 19711
www.speedypublishing.com

The feudal system was the basis for basic government in Medieval Europe. It was used in Europe for several hundred years.

What is the feudal system? It is a system of government in which the people promised their loyalty and service to their lords. The lord could be the lord of the local manor, a regional leader like a duke or an earl, or even the king himself. In return for the people's loyalty and hard work, the nobles protected the people in time of war and let them occupy and use a piece of land.

Feudal System in Medieval Europe. At the top of the feudal system was the monarch, usually the king. The king conducted a vassal ceremony in which every person involved would promise his loyalty to the king. The person would swear to fight for the king.

After the ceremony, the king would give the vassal control of land known as a fief. These persons who received the land were called tenants-in-chief. These nobles or barons swore their services to the king. This was called homage to the king.

People believed that God granted to kings the right to rule. This was called the divine right.

Land was granted to tenants for service. The wealthy tenants-in-chief would pay the king. The educated members of the church or clergymen would give the king advice.

The nobles or barons would send the king soldiers or knights who would defend his kingdom and fight the country's enemies. This was in return for the land granted for them. The king held most of the power and wealth.

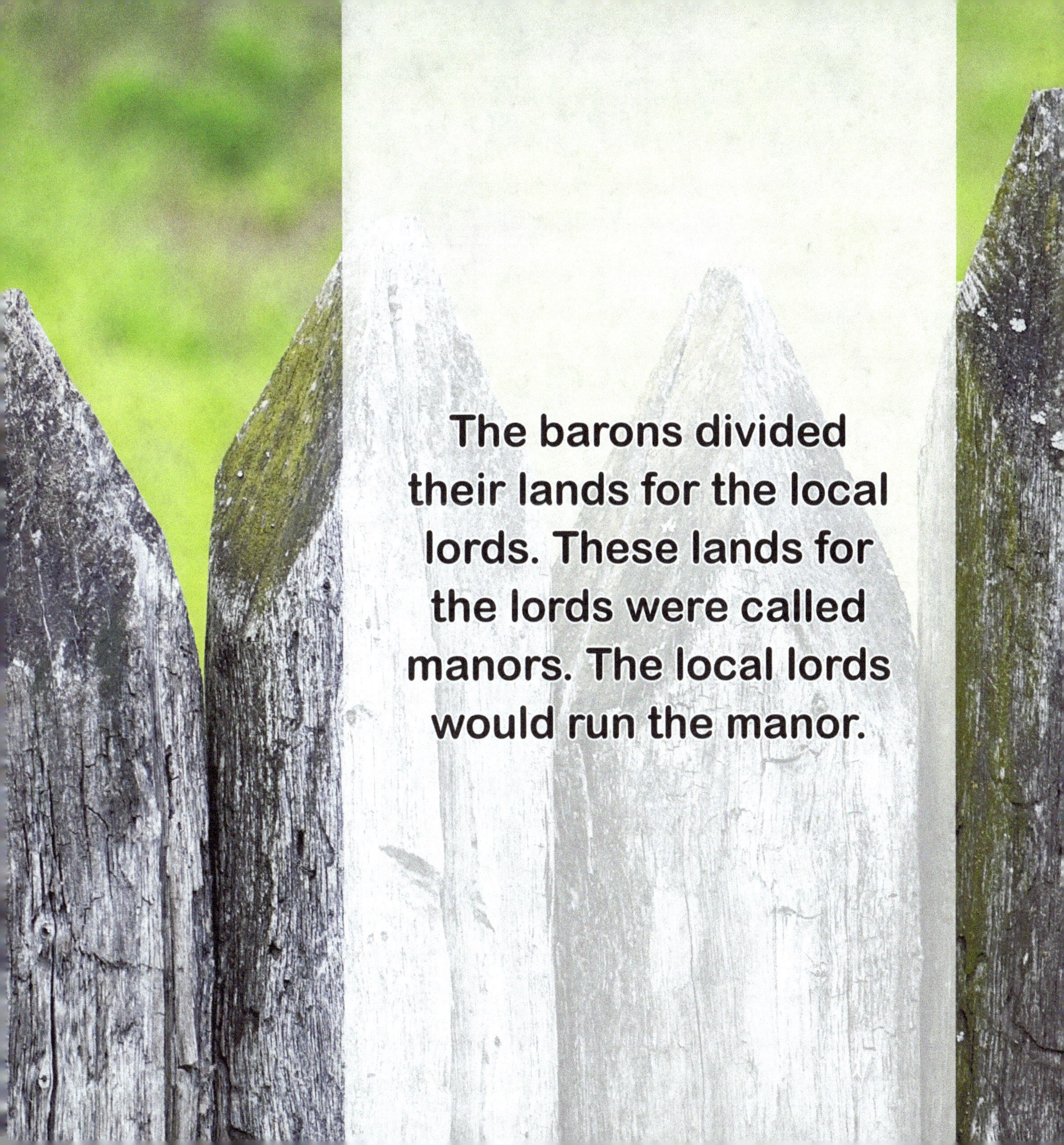

The barons divided their lands for the local lords. These lands for the lords were called manors. The local lords would run the manor.

The knights were given land by the lords. In return, the knights would fight for the king, or as the lord directed. The knights would protect the property fiefdom and the people who lived in it.

The lowest part in the feudal system was the peasants. The peasants were given lands by the lords. They were known as serfs. Serfs worked in the lord or knight's land. These peasants rented their lands.

The peasants planted crops in their rented land. They would pay rent to the lords. Aside from this, the peasants would pay tithes, or a tax of 10% from their earnings, to the Church.

This is what
feudalism is all about.
It is service for land.

What is the Manor in the Feudal System? The manor was the district or a community. It was led by a lord. The lord had the total rights as ruler and judge, and enjoyed wide privileges in it. A manor included the lord's large house or castle. The peasants lived in the village around the castle. Each manor had farmlands, woodlands, and a church.

If the lords could not provide soldiers for the king, they were asked to pay taxes known as shield money. The lord owned almost everything in the manor. He owned the peasants, the farms and the village as a whole.

Who were the peasants? Peasants composed the majority of people in the Middle Ages. They cultivated the land. In return, they were protected by the lord. They were asked to pay taxes and to give the biggest part of their harvest to the lord. Their lives weren't easy.

However, some peasants enjoyed their freedom. These were the skilled few and the business minded people. These people included the bakers, carpenters and blacksmiths.

Other peasants were slaves. They worked hard 6 days a week. They died young because of having to work so hard, often in dangerous tasks.

Women in the feudal system were assigned to household tasks. These tasks included cooking, baking, weaving, spinning, and sewing. Some women also learned to use weapons and fought battles. Some women were well-educated.

Every country in the world today has its own form of government. The leaders of the different countries implemented rules for the people and for the country itself. Feudalism has been replaced almost everywhere.

Visit
BABY PROFESSOR
EDUCATION KIDS
www.BabyProfessorBooks.com
to download Free Baby Professor eBooks and view
our catalog of new and exciting Children's Books

www.ingramcontent.com/pod-product-compliance
Lightning Source LLC
LaVergne TN
LVHW060832170826
845678LV00010B/1958

* 9 7 9 8 8 6 9 4 4 4 0 5 9 *